DATE DUE			

GEORGE WASHINGTON CARVER

Also by Suzanne M. Coil

Florida

George Washington Carver

GEORGE WASHINGTON CARVER

BY SUZANNE M. COIL

FRANKLIN WATTS / A FIRST BOOK / 1990
NEW YORK / LONDON / TORONTO / SYDNEY

Cover photograph courtesy of: Historical Picture Service

Photographs courtesy of: Historical Picture Service: pp. 10, 52;
National Park Service/George Washington Carver National Monument:
pp. 13, 18, 33, 43, 51, 54; Simpson College: p. 23; USDA:
pp. 25, 26, 32, 37, 41; The Bettmann Archive: pp. 31, 35; UPI/Bettmann
Newsphotos: pp. 46, 49 top; AP/Wide World Photos: p. 49 bottom.

Library of Congress Cataloging-in-Publication Data

Coil, Suzanne M.
George Washington Carver / by Suzanne M. Coil.
p.   cm. — (A First book)
Includes bibliographical references.
Summary: Discusses the life, innovations, and accomplishments of
the famous scientist.
ISBN 0-531-10864-3
1. Carver, George Washington, 1864?–1943—Juvenile literature.
2. Afro-American agriculturists—Biography—Juvenile literature.
3. Agriculturists—United States—Biography—Juvenile literature.
[1. Carver, George Washington, 1864?–1943. 2. Scientists. 3. Afro-
Americans—Biography.] I. Title. II. Series.
S417.C3C65   1990
630′.92—dc20
[B]
[92]
90-12283 CIP AC

For Christopher,
With Love

Many thanks to the staff of the George Washington Carver National Monument in Diamond, Missouri, for their courtesy and help in supplying information. The George Washington Carver National Monument, founded in 1943, was the first national park dedicated to the memory of a black American.

CONTENTS

*"My work, my life, must be in
the spirit of a little child seeking only
to know the truth and follow it."*
George Washington Carver

Chapter One

CARVER'S GEORGE

In 1864, in a log cabin on a farm near the small town of Diamond, Missouri, a slave woman named Mary was tending her sick baby. The little boy, whose name was George, had a bad case of whooping cough. Suddenly, the door of the cabin burst open. A group of strange men rushed in. Roughly, they forced Mary and her baby out the door and onto one of the horses waiting outside.

Mary's screams alerted her master, Moses Carver, and his wife, Susan. By the time they reached the cabin, Mary and little George were gone.

At that time, the United States was torn by a bitter war between the North and the South. Slavery was one of the issues dividing the nation.

Throughout the Civil War (1861–1865), people continued to buy and sell slaves. Some men were getting rich by stealing slaves and reselling them. The men who had kidnapped Mary and little George were slave stealers.

The Carvers, who owned Mary and George, had come from Germany to begin a new life in America. They were kindly people who reluctantly accepted the idea of slavery. They treated their slaves like members of the family.

When Mary and her baby were stolen, the Carvers were very upset. Moses Carver hired a man to find them. After searching for several weeks, the man returned, carrying Mary's baby more dead than alive. He said that the baby had been left along the way by the thieves, but that he had found no trace of Mary. She was never heard from again. George's father, who was a slave on a neighboring farm, had died in an accident a few months before. Little George was now an orphan, but he had Moses and Susan Carver.

Susan tenderly nursed Mary's baby as though he were her own. Little George survived, but he was a small, thin child. As he grew older, he was too frail to be of much help to Moses Carver in the fields, so George helped Susan with household jobs instead. She taught him how to cook and clean, how

*Dr. Carver's early home
in Diamond, Missouri*

to wash and iron clothes, and how to sew and knit. Best of all, the Carvers taught George how to read. He was full of curiosity and quickly learned everything that Susan and Moses Carver could teach him.

When his chores were done, George liked nothing better than to roam the meadows and woods nearby. There was so much to discover. His bright eyes noticed everything. It wasn't long before George made friends with every animal, bird, and insect. Every day, he brought home objects he found outdoors so that he could study them more closely. He gathered a fine collection of interesting rocks that he kept throughout his life.

Of all the things that George discovered, the most fascinating of all were plants. Deep in the woods, he made a secret garden where he planted wildflowers and unusual plants gathered during his walks. As George watched his garden grow, his mind was filled with a million questions. Why were some flowers red and others blue or white or yellow? Why did some grow tall and others stay small? Why did some grow better in sunshine, while others grew best in shady places? Why did some wither and die, while others remained healthy? Why? Why? Why? George tended his garden carefully, hoping that the plants would tell him their secrets.

By the time George was eight years old, he had learned a great deal about plants by patiently trying simple experiments in his secret garden. He grew plants in various mixtures of clay, sand, and loam (soil made of clay, sand, silt, and organic matter), and gave them different amounts of water and sunlight in order to discover which combination was best for each kind of plant. George watched insects closely to see which ones caused damage to plants. People started talking about George and his plant magic. They nicknamed him "the Plant Doctor" and called on him to cure their sickly plants.

Although George learned a lot by himself, there was still so much he didn't know. He pestered the Carvers with questions about all sorts of things. Sometimes they knew the answers, but often they didn't. George asked if he might go to Neosho, a town eight miles away, where there was a school for black children. Moses Carver gave his permission, but the Carvers were poor and had no money to help George pay the school fees.

There was one thing, however, that Moses Carver could give to the little boy: his name. In the days of slavery, slaves had only first names. When the Civil War ended in 1865, many newly freed slaves adopted the last names of their former owners.

During his early life, George was known as "Carver's George."

When he was ten years old, George set out on his own. He arrived in Neosho, Missouri, late one night, without a penny in his pocket and no place to live, but with the brand-new name of George Carver. The first thing he did was to find the schoolhouse. Right next door, he saw a small house and barn. George crept into the barn and went to sleep on a pile of hay. The next morning, he was discovered by the people who lived in the house. That is how he met Mariah and Andrew Watkins, who became very important to him.

The Watkinses were a religious black couple who had no children of their own. The sight of the skinny boy with the bright, dark eyes touched Mariah deeply, and she offered to take George in. In return for her kindness, George worked hard helping Mariah with her laundry chores. In the evening, Mariah and Andrew enjoyed listening to George read the Bible aloud to them.

For the next three years, George lived with the Watkinses and attended the Lincoln School. From Mariah, George learned how to make various kinds of medicines using herbs and wild plants. But school was disappointing to George. When he realized that he knew more about most things than his teachers did, he decided it was time to move on.

George had grown to love the Watkinses. It was hard to leave them, but his hunger to learn drove him on. When some neighbors announced that they were moving to Fort Scott, Kansas, a bustling town that had several schools, George arranged to ride along with the family.

George was thirteen years old when he enrolled in school at Fort Scott. He worked at odd jobs, earning just enough to keep from starving. He read every book and newspaper he could lay his hands on. In his spare time, he practiced drawing pictures. George decided that he wanted to study art and become an artist someday.

His life was lonely, and when some white classmates tormented him and destroyed his schoolbooks, he tasted the cruelty of racial prejudice. But poor and lonely as George was, he was still happy because he was learning something new every day. Then, something terrible happened, something so awful that it haunted him for the rest of his life.

On the evening of March 26, 1879, George watched in horror as an angry mob of white men dragged a black man out of the Fort Scott jail. After beating the man badly, the gang threw kerosene

on his body and set fire to it. George packed his few belongings and ran from the town that night. He never forgot the sight of the lynching or the terrible smell of burning flesh.

George knew then that he wanted to do something important with his life, something of value that would help his fellow black people. He would have to decide what that "something" would be.

Carver had decided at an early age that he liked painting, and he decided to study art.

Chapter Two

"WE DON'T TAKE NEGROES HERE"

George was fifteen years old when he left Fort Scott. He traveled from one small town to another, attending school and supporting himself by doing laundry and cooking wherever he went. In 1885, he graduated from high school. But George's hungry mind still buzzed with questions. He decided to go to college.

George nearly burst with happiness when the letter came saying that he was admitted to Highland College in Kansas. That summer he worked hard to save up money for college. And he took a trip to visit Moses and Susan Carver. The Carvers' "little George" was now six feet tall. They hugged and kissed him. When he left, they gave him his mother Mary's spinning wheel as a remembrance. It was the last time he ever saw his white "parents."

George arrived at Highland that fall, happy and eager to learn. But when he went to register for classes, the college official looked with surprise at George's dark face. "There's been a mistake," the man said. "We don't take Negroes here. Never have, and never will." George turned away, badly hurt and bitterly disappointed. It seemed as though his world was coming to an end. What was a poor, young black man to do?

Someone told George that cheap land was available in Ness County, Kansas. Maybe farming was the answer. Plants had always been his dearest friends, and now that the world seemed to be rejecting him, he turned to them for comfort.

In 1886, George Washington Carver filed a claim on a homestead. (He took Washington for his middle name about this time.) He built himself a house of sod (grass-covered soil held together by roots) and began to raise crops and conduct agricultural experiments in the hard soil of the prairie. The farmers nearby soon realized that their gentle, modest black neighbor was a very special person. They admired his drawings and paintings and invited him to parties and dances. George made many friends in Ness County, but after a few years, he knew that it was time to move on.

George sold the farm and went to Winterset, Iowa. One day, while singing at a church service, he was noticed by Dr. and Mrs. John Milholland. The Milhollands soon realized that George had a brilliant, sensitive mind. They urged him to enroll at nearby Simpson College. George told them what had happened at Highland and that he was afraid of being rejected. But the Milhollands encouraged him to try again. This time, George listened. He had felt for a long time that God meant him to do something special with his life. Maybe at Simpson College, he would find his way.

After George paid the twelve-dollar tuition at Simpson, he had only ten cents left. In an abandoned shack near the campus, he set up a laundry business to earn enough money for food and books. One of his teachers said later, "George Carver came to us with a satchel full of poverty and a burning zeal to know everything." At Simpson, George studied art and produced many beautiful paintings of flowers and plants. His teachers told him that he could become a great artist, but he felt that God had other plans for him.

Once, when he was still a little boy, George had wanted a pocketknife more than anything, but had

*This rare photograph of George Washington
Carver shows him in an art class with
several other students at Simpson College.*

no money to buy one. One night he dreamed he saw a pocketknife sticking in a watermelon lying in a field. The next morning he ran to the field, and there, just as he'd seen it in the dream, was the pocketknife stuck in a watermelon.

While George was a student at Simpson, dreams like this returned to him. His nighttime visions convinced him that God wanted him to teach something useful to his fellow blacks. Along with his dreams, the influence of an art teacher at Simpson, Etta Budd, caused George to switch his studies to agriculture and enroll at Iowa State College of Agriculture and Mechanic Arts.

Back once more with his beloved plants, George studied botany, chemistry, and plant diseases. He experimented with cross-breeding, hybridizing, and grafting. He became an expert mycologist, a person who knows all about mushrooms and fungi. When George graduated in 1894, his professors

Although he enjoyed painting and drawing, Carver decided to study botany instead. Here he is doing an experiment with cabbages.

Some of George Washington Carver's classmates at Iowa State. He enjoyed his studies there very much.

offered him a job as a teacher and asked him to be head of the college greenhouses. They urged him to work for a Master of Science degree. George loved his friends at Iowa State and he loved working with his plants. He agreed to stay.

He wrote pamphlets telling farmers how to fight plant diseases and grow better crops. Soon scientists around the country became aware of George's experiments with plants.

Then, one day, in May 1896, the postman brought a letter that was to change George's life. The letter came from Booker T. Washington, a young black man who had started a school in Tuskegee, Alabama. He planned to teach black people the knowledge and skills they needed to earn a living. Most of the black people in the South were farmers, and Tuskegee desperately needed someone to teach agriculture. Washington begged George Carver to teach at Tuskegee. "I cannot offer you money, position or fame," he wrote. "I offer you in their place work—hard, hard work—the task of bringing a people from degradation, poverty and waste to full manhood."

At last, George knew what he was meant to do!

Chapter Three

'WAY DOWN SOUTH IN DIXIE

When George arrived at Tuskegee in the fall of 1896, he was surprised by what he found. He'd expected to see a laboratory, a dairy, and a greenhouse. But the "dairy" consisted of a single cow, his "laboratory" was an empty room, and there was no greenhouse at all. The school was housed in a few bare buildings surrounded by acres of hard, ugly clay. "I had never seen anything like it," he said later. "There was yellow soil and red and purple and brown and riveted and banded, and all sorts of things, except grass or plants. There were erosion gullies in which an ox could get lost!"

George was even more troubled by what he saw in the countryside around Tuskegee. Everywhere he looked, he saw poor people, both black and white. His heart ached on seeing the signs of hunger in the faces of the skinny, barefoot children. Why were these farmers so poor? George knew the answer when he saw the stunted cotton plants growing in the fields.

Cotton, the crop that had once brought wealth to the area, had wasted the land. Cotton plants drain the soil of its minerals. After several harvests, the soil becomes eroded and barren. But Alabama farmers continued to grow cotton because it was the only crop that they could sell for profit. Large planters burned down thousands of acres of forests to gain new, fertile land. When that soil was worn out, they abandoned it and went on to burn more forests. Small farmers couldn't afford to move on. They stayed on their land, becoming poorer and poorer as their fields produced less and less cotton. Many became so poor that they lost their farms and had to work as tenant farmers or field hands for someone else.

George's students had grown up on farms such as these. They came to Tuskegee hoping to learn useful skills and trades that would allow them to escape the poverty of farm life. George was discouraged to learn that farming was the last thing in the world they wanted to study. He would have to find a way to change their minds.

George soon realized that a huge task lay ahead of him. Not only would he have to encourage and motivate his students, he would have to find a way to help the poor farmers in the area as well.

First, George needed to outfit his laboratory. The school had no money to spend, so George set to work making equipment from old bottles, jars, and other throwaways. He sent his students to search scrap heaps for discarded pots, pans, lamps, jar lids, rubber, or anything else that might be useful.

When the makeshift laboratory was ready, George began testing samples of the soil around Tuskegee to find out what it was made of and what minerals it needed to make it fertile.

His students wondered what this strange, slender man from the North was up to. He wasn't going to teach them farming, he told them. They were going to learn "scientific agriculture." He explained that some plants, such as cotton, use up the minerals in soil, but by growing pod-bearing plants, minerals could be restored to the soil. He promised to show them how.

With his students' help, George plowed up twenty acres around the school and planted cowpeas—a plant that would give the soil some of the minerals it needed. When people saw what George had done, they thought he was crazy. Cowpeas were only good

Dr. Carver was a talented and inspiring teacher to his students. Here he is instructing some students in his lab at Tuskegee.

Throughout his career, Dr. Carver was always experimenting and learning about new things. As a teacher, he believed in hands-on activities for his pupils.

for hog feed! But when the peas were picked, George cooked them into a delicious meal. His students were surprised to learn how good cowpeas could taste.

Next, George and his students planted sweet potatoes. Again, people laughed. But they stopped laughing when they saw the huge sweet potato harvest.

"We've been rotating crops on this land," George told his students. "The soil has been rested, refreshed, and enriched. Now we'll plant cotton."

The country people had already decided that George was a "root doctor" because they had seen him gathering weeds, roots, bark, and flowers in nearby woods and swamps. They had come to him with their aches and pains, and he had shown them how to brew healing teas and how to use vitamin-rich weeds to enrich their diets. Now they came

George Washington Carver never stopped experimenting with new crops to find better growing methods and uses for products.

from miles around to gaze in wonder at the bursting bolls of cotton ripening on strong, sturdy stems. "Doctor" Carver must be a plant magician, they said. They were ready to listen to anything George might tell them about growing cotton.

Since it was hard for many of the country people to come to Tuskegee to see George, he decided to go to them instead. He outfitted a wagon with farm implements and exhibits, and with some of his students, drove the "Movable School of Agriculture" from town to town. He showed farm families how to make and use organic fertilizer, how to plant and cultivate their crops, how to treat plant diseases, how to cook and preserve food by canning and drying, how to tend fruit trees, and much more.

People listened to George. Soon the fields of Alabama were filled with lovely cotton blossoms. The farmers who had learned to rotate their crops and "rest" their soil looked forward to the best cotton harvest in years.

Then, in one night, a terrible thing happened. The snowy cotton blossoms turned brown and fell to the ground. The cotton plants withered and drooped. The boll weevil, a little worm that had eaten its way through cotton fields from Mexico to Mississippi, had arrived in Alabama. The cotton

*For the farmers and their families who came
to Tuskegee, Carver lectured on how to farm
more efficiently. Here he is talking at a
farmers' conference at the university.*

crop was destroyed. Without a cash crop to depend on, country people faced ruin and hunger.

The farmers begged George to help them. He told them that there was no way to get rid of boll weevils. The best thing to do, he said, was to plow under the cotton and plant peanuts instead. "What will we do with goobers?" they asked. (Goobers was their name for peanuts.) "Goobers are only good for animals!"

George explained that peanuts were an ideal food for people. He told farmers how to cultivate, harvest, and use them. All the advice George had given them in the past had worked out fine, so once again they listened to him. They planted peanuts. But when it came time to sell their peanuts, they discovered that no one wanted to buy them.

People began to ask themselves why they had ever listened to that young man at Tuskegee. Farmers who had once begged him for help now blamed George for all their troubles. But no one blamed him more than he blamed himself.

George told himself that this disaster was his own fault. Slowly, his thin shoulders sagging, he went into his laboratory and shut the door.

Chapter Four

A POCKETFUL OF GOOBERS

George shut the door of "God's little workshop" (the name he called his laboratory) and took a handful of peanuts from his pocket. He had to work fast. But first he prayed. "Please, Mr. Creator," he asked, "will you tell me why the peanut was made?"

Day and night, for nearly a week, George stayed locked in his laboratory. His students were worried. Was he all right? When they knocked on the door, he answered in a strange voice, "Go away. We're busy!"

At last, he opened the door and invited his students in. He told them that the "Great Creator" had taught him how to take the peanut apart chemically and put the separate parts together again in new and different ways. Peanuts, he explained, were packed with protein, carbohydrates, and vitamins. He showed the students how he had combined and recombined the oils, sugars, starches, and other elements he discovered in peanuts to produce two dozen new products including cooking oil, rubbing oil, milk, cheese, and margarine.

George decided that if people knew about these new uses for peanuts, then farmers would be able to sell their peanut crops. To convince local businessmen that a demand could be created for peanut products, George invited them to lunch at Tuskegee. The menu included soup, bread, "chicken" loaf, vegetables, ice cream, and cookies. After his guests finished the delicious meal, George announced that everything they had eaten had been made from peanuts!

The businessmen were so enthusiastic about George's discoveries that they founded in 1919 in Atlanta, Georgia, the United Peanut Associations of America. Soon the association had hundreds of members, and George was invited to address the group's first annual meeting.

With a crate packed full of exhibits, George arrived at the City Hall in Montgomery, Alabama, where the meeting was being held. A sign over the door said "No Colored," and the doorman refused to let George in. He was deeply hurt, but he

*Dr. Carver with peanuts and products
from the nut. He discovered over
three hundred uses for the peanut.*

didn't go away. He was there to help poor farmers, both black and white, who lived in what he called "the lowlands of sorrow." After managing to send a note inside, he was finally admitted.

George told the audience about his work with peanuts. Everyone was amazed when he showed them the things he had made from peanuts—milk drinks, cheeses, stains and dyes, linoleum, peanut butter, and so much more! When an Alabama congressman in the audience suggested that Professor Carver should represent the peanut growers before Congress at the upcoming hearings on protective tariffs, everyone cheered.

On January 20, 1921, George carried his heavy wooden crate up the steps of the Capitol building in Washington, D.C. Most of the congressmen thought that it was silly to include peanuts in the tariff bill. After all, peanuts weren't good for anything. They thought it would be a waste of time to listen to the thin, stooped black man in the rumpled clothes who was making his way to the front of the room. They told him he had ten minutes to speak. But after the ten minutes were up, everyone was so interested in what George had to say that they told him to take as much time as he needed.

Two more
products the
scientist made
from peanuts:
peanut meal and
vanishing cream
for the skin.

"The peanut," George said, "is one of the most remarkable crops. . . . It has possibilities that we are just beginning to find out." He talked about his experiments and showed some of the samples in his crate: several kinds of candy bars and breakfast foods, various kinds of animal and bird feed, ice cream powder, peanut meal, flour, thirty different dyes made from peanut skins, a substance for burnishing tin plate made from peanut hulls, milk, margarine, cream, buttermilk, Worcestershire sauce, pickles, sauces, cheeses, oils, cosmetics and beauty creams, inks, relishes, a coffee substitute—the list went on and on.

By the time George was finished, he had convinced the congressmen that the lowly peanut was a valuable crop. They voted to help peanut farmers by putting a high tariff on peanuts imported from other countries. This meant that the farmers could get a good price for their peanuts.

Newspapers all over the country carried the story of George's speech. People were amazed to learn that peanuts could be used in so many ways. Suddenly, George Washington Carver, the gentle scientist from Tuskegee, was famous.

Chapter Five

THE GENTLE WIZARD OF TUSKEGEE

Back at Tuskegee, George was busier than ever. Invitations to speak poured in. He was showered with awards and honorary degrees.

Henry Ford and Thomas Alva Edison, the famous inventors, became his friends. Edison offered to pay George a great deal of money and give him a completely equipped laboratory if George would go to work for him. But George refused. He said he would remain at Tuskegee where he could "be of the greatest good to the greatest number of 'my people.' "

Although he might have become very wealthy, George refused to accept money for his discoveries. To businessmen who offered to pay him for the rights to use his formulas, George said, "The

Lord charges me nothing for my knowledge. I will charge you the same." And to people who asked for his advice, he said, "If I know the answer, you can have it for the price of a postage stamp."

Money meant nothing to George. Throughout his nearly fifty years at Tuskegee, he earned only $125 a month. He turned down every offer of a raise in pay. "It is not the style of clothes one wears, neither the kind of automobile one drives, nor the amount of money one has in the bank that counts. These mean nothing," he said. "It is simply service that measures success."

George lived very simply in two small rooms. In his spare time he painted pictures, using paints he made from Alabama soils. He even made his own ties, mended his shoes, and knitted his own socks! He owned one shabby, worn-out suit. When his friends urged him to buy a new suit now that he

Henry Ford gave Dr. Carver a modern, fully equipped laboratory for food research. Guests at the ceremony in 1942 ate sandwiches and salads made by Dr. Carver from weeds and wild vegetables.

was famous, he insisted that he didn't need another one. But every morning, he put a fresh flower in the buttonhole of his jacket.

Despite the fame and honors heaped on him, George continued to spend long hours at work. Altogether, he discovered more than three hundred valuable uses for the peanut plant. One of his most astounding discoveries was how peanut oil could be used to help children crippled by infantile paralysis. (These were the days before the polio vaccine.) Parents brought their crippled children and doctors sent their small patients to George. His work contributed to the search for other effective methods of treatment.

But George's research didn't stop with peanuts. He studied sweet potatoes, another crop important to poor farmers, and developed 118 products that could be made from them. He developed a new, sturdy kind of cotton, and showed how cotton could be used to make paving blocks, paper, rugs, insulating boards, and many other products. He developed various kinds of fertilizers and showed farmers how to use them to improve their crops. He analyzed Alabama clay, and from it he made paints, stains, and face powder. The crayons that children use are colored with pigments that George discovered in clay.

President Franklin D. Roosevelt pays a visit to Tuskegee Institute and meets with Dr. Carver.

Thousands of people suffering from polio wrote to Dr. Carver to thank him for his achievement in the extraction of an oil from peanuts for use in the treatment of the disease.

During World War II, many of George's discoveries, such as plastics made of soybeans and rubber made from sludge, were important because they could be used in place of materials that were scarce or unavailable. Because he was the first scientist to develop such products, he is called the "Father of Synthetics."

But George was not only a great scientist, he was a great teacher as well. George loved his students. They were his family, and they loved him in return.

Everything in nature has a purpose, George told them, and it is the scientist's job to find out what that purpose is and then put it to good use to help people. He urged his students to think for themselves and to look at old ideas in new ways. "Young people," he said, "I want to beg of you, always keep your eyes and ears open to what Mother Nature has to teach you. By so doing you will learn many valuable things every day of your life." He often quoted his favorite Bible verse: "Behold, I have given you every herb bearing seed, which is upon

Dr. Carver was known as the "Wizard of Tuskegee."

the face of all the earth . . . to you it shall be for meat."

George taught his students how to transform plants such as peanuts, sweet potatoes, cowpeas, and soybeans into "meat," and how to make useful things from "useless" weeds and materials that were ordinarily thrown away. It was a crime, he said, to see poor people going hungry when there were riches all around them waiting to be discovered and used.

George began each day by taking a long walk, stopping to examine plants, stones, soil, and insects along the way. The years passed, and now he was seventy-nine years old. One day, he felt too sick to get up. He didn't want to be sick. "I still have work to do!" he complained.

But on January 5, 1943, "Mr. Creator" decided that George Washington Carver's work was done.

In 1939 Dr. Carver received the Roosevelt Medal, established in 1923 to honor people who have distinguished themselves in fields associated with the career of President Theodore Roosevelt.

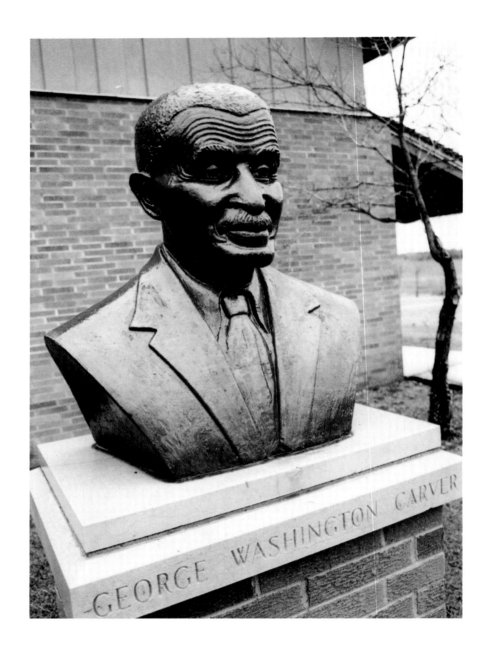

He had spent his life teaching the children of ex-slaves like himself and working hard to help "the man farthest down." His discoveries had revitalized agriculture in the South, and given new hope to millions.

Hundreds of poor people, both black and white, came to say good-bye to their friend. They buried George Washington Carver at Tuskegee, surrounded by mounds of sweet flowers. He was wearing his old suit with a fresh blossom in his buttonhole.

Forty years of creative research were commemorated with the unveiling of a bronze bust of George Washington Carver in June 1937 at Tuskegee Institute.

ACTIVITIES AND EXPERIMENTS

George Washington Carver's lifelong career as a scientist began during his childhood. Here are some interesting activities and experiments for you to try.

Make Your Own Peanut Butter

✱ Put 2 cups of roasted salted peanuts into an electric blender. Put a cover on the blender, and blend the peanuts on medium speed for about a minute. Then blend on high speed for a few seconds more. Stop the blender. Use a spoon or spatula to push unbroken or large chunks of peanuts toward the center of the blender, being careful not to cut yourself on the blender blades. Put the cover back on, and blend some more on high speed. Keep doing this until the peanuts are ground into a smooth paste.

If you don't have a blender, you can grind the peanuts by hand, using a mortar and pestle. This is hard work—but it's the way George Washington Carver made peanut butter! Place the peanut butter in a covered glass jar and store it in the refrigerator for a few days. Notice the layer of peanut oil that rises to the top of the jar. Now stir the oil back into the mashed peanuts. When it is thoroughly mixed, you are ready to eat your peanut butter. Spread some on a piece of bread, add jelly if you like, and enjoy a great American treat. But watch out. This natural peanut butter *will* stick to the roof of your mouth!

Grow a Sweet Potato (or Yam) Vine
Stick 5 or 6 toothpicks around the middle of a sweet potato. Put some water into a clean jar. Suspend one end of the sweet potato in the water by letting the toothpicks rest on the rim of the jar. Place the jar on a sunny windowsill. In a few days, you will see roots begin to form on the part of the sweet potato that is in the water. Leaves will begin to form on the upper part of the potato. In a few weeks, you will have a lovely sweet potato vine. Just remember to add water to the jar every now and then. The leaves of the sweet potato vine can be eaten, and are delicious when cooked like spinach or other greens.

Grow an Egg Carton Garden

For this project, you will need a cardboard egg carton. (Do not use a carton made of plastic.) Also, you will need some seeds. Flower seeds, such as those of zinnias or marigolds, or bean seeds work well.

Cut the base of a cardboard egg carton in half. You now have 2 "planters" with 6 "pots" in each. Next, fill the pots with soil. Plant a few seeds in each pot and cover them with a thin layer of soil. Pour a little water into each pot. Now place one of the planters on a sunny windowsill. Place the second planter in a dark or shady location. Check the soil in the planters every day. If the soil feels dry, add a little water. In a few days, you will begin to see baby plants sprouting in one of the planters. Which one? Are the seeds in the second planter sprouting? If not, why?

Move the second planter to the sunny windowsill. Keep checking to see if the seeds sprout. Do they? Why?

When your plants are a few inches high, you can cut the pots apart and plant them directly in larger flowerpots or, if it is warm outdoors, you can plant them in your garden. You don't have to take the plants out of their cardboard pots, because the cardboard will eventually decompose into the soil. Remember to water your plants. In a few weeks, you will be able to enjoy your flowers (or beans)!

Nature Drawings
George Washington Carver drew and painted many beautiful pictures of plants. Draw or paint pictures of some plants that you like. Pay close attention to the shapes and colors of the leaves, stems, and flowers. Try to draw them as exactly as you can. Collect your drawings in a notebook.

Nature Walk
Take a walk around your school. How many different kinds of plants do you see? Don't forget to count the weeds and trees!

FOR
FURTHER READING

Adair, Gene. *George Washington Carver, Botanist*. New York: Chelsea House, 1989.

Graham, Shirley, and George D. Lipscomb. *Dr. George Washington Carver, Scientist*. New York: Julian Messner, 1971.

Kremer, Gary R. *George Washington Carver: In His Own Words*. Columbia: University of Missouri Press, 1987.

Mitchell, Barbara. *A Pocketful of Goobers: A Story about George Washington Carver*. Minneapolis: Carolrhoda Books, 1986.

INDEX

ABOUT
THE AUTHOR

Since the age of fourteen, when she went to work as a part-time newspaper reporter and columnist, Suzanne M. Coil has been devoted to writing and books. She worked for many years in book publishing in New York, and has also taught writing to college students. Her books for young readers include *Florida* and *The Poor in America*. She is currently working on a biography of Harriet Beecher Stowe for young adults. Ms. Coil and her husband, Jesse, live in Covington, Louisiana.